The Kingdom of Love

Ella Wheeler Wilcox

The Kingdom of Love

Copyright © 2019 Indo-European Publishing

The present edition is a reproduction of previous publication of this classic work. Minor typographical errors may have been corrected without note, however, for an authentic reading experience the spelling, punctuation, and capitalization have been retained from the original text.

ISBN: 978-1-64439-211-9

CONTENTS

THE KINGDOM OF LOVE

In the dawn of the day when the sea and the earth
   Reflected the sunrise above,
I set forth with a heart full of courage and mirth
   To seek for the Kingdom of Love.
I asked of a Poet I met on the way
   Which cross-road would lead me aright;
And he said "Follow me, and ere long you shall see
   Its glittering turrets of light."

And soon in the distance a city shone fair.
   "Look yonder," he said; "How it gleams!"
But alas! for the hopes that were doomed to despair,
   It was only the "Kingdom of Dreams."
Then the next man I asked was a gay Cavalier,
   And he said: "Follow me, follow me";
And with laughter and song we went speeding along
   By the shores of Life's beautiful sea.

Then we came to a valley more tropical far
   Than the wonderful vale of Cashmere,
And I saw from a bower a face like a flower
   Smile out on the gay Cavalier;
And he said: "We have come to humanity's goal:
   Here love and delight are intense."
But alas and alas! for the hopes of my soul—
   It was only the "Kingdom of Sense."

As I journeyed more slowly I met on the road
   A coach with retainers behind;

And they said: "Follow me, for our Lady's abode
　　Belongs in that realm, you will find."
'Twas a grand dame of fashion, a newly-made bride,
　　I followed, encouraged and bold;
But my hopes died away like the last gleams of day,
　　For we came to the "Kingdom of Gold."

At the door of a cottage I asked a fair maid.
　　"I have heard of that realm," she replied;
"But my feet never roam from the 'Kingdom of Home,'
　　So I know not the way," and she sighed.
I looked on the cottage; how restful it seemed!
　　And the maid was as fair as a dove.
Great light glorified my soul as I cried:
　　"Why, Home is the 'Kingdom of Love'!"

MEG'S CURSE

The sun rode high in a cloudless sky
    Of a perfect summer morn.
She stood and gazed out into the street,
    And wondered why she was born.
On the topmost branch of a maple-tree
    That close by the window grew,
A robin called to his mate enthralled:
    "I love but you, but you, but you."

A soft look came in her hardened face—
    She had not wept for years;
But the robin's trill, as some sounds will,
    Jarred open the door of tears.
She thought of the old home far away;
    She heard the whr-r-r of the mill;
She heard the turtle's wild, sweet call,
        And the wail of the whip-poor-will, whip-poor-will, whip-
poor-will.

She saw again that dusty road
    Whence he came riding down;
She smelled once more the flower she wore
    In the breast of her simple gown.
Out on the new-mown meadow she heard
    Two blue-jays quarrel and fret,
And the warning cry of a Phoebe bird
    "More wet, more wet, more wet."

With a blithe "Hello" to the men below
  Who were spreading the new-mown hay,
The rider drew rein at her window-pane—
  How it all came back to-day!
How young she was, and how fair she was;
  What innocence crowned her brow!
The future seemed fair, for Love was there—
  And now—and now—and now.

In a dingy glass on the wall near by
  She gazed on her faded face.
"Well, Meg, I declare, what a beauty you are!
  She sneered, "What an angel of grace!
Ha, ha, ha, ha, ha, ha, ha, ha!
  What a thing of beauty and grace!"
She reached out her arms with a moaning sob:
  "Oh, if I could go back!"
Then, swift and strange, came a sudden change;
  Her brow grew hard and black.

"A curse on the day and a curse on that man,
  And on all who are his," she cried;
"May he starve and be cold, may he live to be old
  When all who loved him have died."
Her wild voice frightened the robin away
  From the branch by the window-sill;
And little he knew as away he flew,
  Of the memories stirred by his trill.

He called to his mate on the grass below,
  "Follow me," as he soared on high;
And as mates have done since the world begun
  She followed, and asked not why.
The dingy room seemed curtained with gloom;
  Meg shivered with nameless dread.

The ghost of her youth and her murdered truth
   Seemed risen up from the dead.

She hurried out into the noisy street,
   For the silence made her afraid;
To flee from thought was all she sought,
   She cared not whither she strayed.
Still on she pressed in her wild unrest
   Up avenues skirting the park,
Where fashion's throng moved gayly along
   In Vanity Fair—when hark!

A clatter of hoofs down the stony street,
   The snort of a frightened horse
That was running wild, and a laughing child
   At play in its very course.
With one swift glance Meg saw it all.
   "His child—my God! his child!"
She cried aloud, as she rushed through the crowd
   Like one grown suddenly wild.

There, almost under the iron feet,
   Hemmed in by a passing cart,
Stood the baby boy—the pride and joy
   Of the man who had broken her heart.
Past swooning women and shouting men
   She fled like a flash of light;
With her slender arm she gathered from harm
   The form of the laughing sprite.

The death-shod feet of the mad horse beat
   Her down on the pavings grey;
But the baby laughed out with a merry shout,
   And thought it splendid play.
He pulled her gown and called to her: "Say,

Dit up and do dat some more,
Das jus' ze way my papa play
  Wiz me on ze nursery floor."

When the frightened father reached the scene,
  His boy looked up and smiled
From the stiffening fold of the arm, death-cold,
  Of Meg, who had died for his child.
Oh! idle words are a woman's curse
  Who loves as woman can;
For put to the test, she will bare her breast
  And die for the sake of the man.

SOLITUDE

Laugh, and the world laughs with you:
Weep, and you weep alone;
  For the sad old earth
  Must borrow its mirth,
It has trouble enough of its own.

Sing, and the hills will answer;
Sigh, it is lost on the air;
  The echoes bound
  To a joyful sound,
But shrink from voicing care.

Rejoice, and men will seek you;
Grieve, and they turn and go;
  They want full measure
  Of all your pleasure,
But they do not want your woe.

Be glad, and your friends are many;
Be sad, and you lose them all;
  There are none to decline
  Your nectared wine,
But alone you must drink life's gall.

Feast, and your halls are crowded;
Fast, and the world goes by;
  Succeed and give,

And it helps you live,
But it cannot help you die.

There is room in the halls of pleasure
For a long and lordly train;
   But one by one
   We must all file on
Through the narrow aisles of pain.

THE GOSSIPS

A rose in my garden, the sweetest and fairest,
  Was hanging her head through the long golden hours;
And early one morning I saw her tears falling,
  And heard a low gossiping talk in the bowers.
The yellow Nasturtium, a spinster all faded,
  Was telling a Lily what ailed the poor Rose:
"That wild roving Bee who was hanging about her,
  Has jilted her squarely, as every one knows.

"I knew when he came, with his singing and sighing,
  His airs and his speeches so fine and so sweet,
Just how it would end; but no one would believe me,
  For all were quite ready to fall at his feet."
"Indeed, you are wrong," said the Lily-belle proudly,
  "I cared nothing for him; he called on me once,
And would have come often, no doubt, if I'd asked him,
  But though he was handsome, I thought him a dunce."

"Now, now, that's not true," cried the tall Oleander.
  "He has travelled and seen every flower that grows;
And one who has supped in the garden of princes,
  We all might have known would not we with the Rose."
"But wasn't she proud when he showed her attention?
  And she let him caress her," said sly Mignonette;
"And I used to see it and blush for her folly.
  The silly thing thinks he will come to her yet."

9

"I thought he was splendid," said pretty pert Larkspur,
   "So dark, and so grand with that gay cloak of gold;
But he tried once to kiss me, the impudent fellow!
   And I got offended; I thought him too bold."
"Oh, fie!" laughed the Almond, "that does for a story.
   Though I hang down my head, yet I see all that goes;
And I saw you reach out trying hard to detain him,
   But he just tapped your cheek and flew by to the Rose.

"He cared nothing for her; he only was flirting
   To while away time, as I very well knew;
So I turned a cold shoulder on all his advances,
   Because I was certain his heart was untrue."
"The Rose is served right for her folly in trusting
   An oily-tongued stranger," quoth proud Columbine.
"I knew what he was, and thought once I would warn her,
   But of course the affair was no business of mine."

"Oh, well," cried the Peony, shrugging her shoulders,
   "I saw all along that the Bee was a flirt;
But the Rose has been always so praised and so petted,
   I thought a good lesson would do her no hurt."
Just then came the sound of a love-song sung sweetly,
   I saw my proud Rose lifting up her bowed head;
And the talk of the gossips was hushed in a moment,
   And the flowers all listened to hear what was said.

And the dark, handsome Bee, with his cloak o'er his
shoulder,
   Came swift through the sunlight and kissed the sad Rose,
And whispered: "My darling, I've roved the world over,
   And you are the loveliest flower that grows."

PLATONIC

I knew it the first of the summer,
  I knew it the same at the end,
That you and your love were plighted,
  But couldn't you be my friend?
Couldn't we sit in the twilight,
  Couldn't we walk on the shore
With only a pleasant friendship
  To bind us, and nothing more?

There was not a word of folly
  Spoken between us two,
Though we lingered oft in the garden
  Till the roses were wet with dew.
We touched on a thousand subjects—
  The moon and the worlds above,—
And our talk was tinctured with science,
  And everything else, save love.

A wholly Platonic friendship
  You said I had proven to you
Could bind a man and a woman
  The whole long season through,
With never a thought of flirting,
  Though both were in their youth
What would you have said, my lady,
  If you had known the truth!

What would you have done, I wonder,
  Had I gone on my knees to you

And told you my passionate story,
  There in the dusk and the dew?
My burning, burdensome story,
  Hidden and hushed so long—
My story of hopeless loving—
  Say, would you have thought it wrong?

But I fought with my heart and conquered,
  I hid my wound from sight;
You were going away in the morning,
  And I said a calm good-night.
But now when I sit in the twilight,
  Or when I walk by the sea
That friendship, quite Platonic,
  Comes surging over me.

And a passionate longing fills me
  For the roses, the dusk, the dew;
For the beautiful summer vanished,
  For the moonlight walks—and you.

GRANDPA'S CHRISTMAS

In his great cushioned chair by the fender
  An old man sits dreaming to-night,
His withered hands, licked by the tender
  Warm rays of the red anthracite,
Are folded before him, all listless;
  His dim eyes are fixed on the blaze,
While over him sweeps the resistless
  Flood-tide of old days.

He hears not the mirth in the hallway,
  He hears not the sounds of good cheer,
That through the old homestead ring alway
  In the glad Christmas-time of the year.
He heeds not the chime of sweet voices
  As the last gifts are hung on the tree.
In a long-vanished day he rejoices—
  In his lost Used-to-be.

He has gone back across dead Decembers
  To his childhood's fair land of delight;
And his mother's sweet smile he remembers,
  As he hangs up his stocking at night.
He remembers the dream-haunted slumber
  All broken and restless because
Of the visions that came without number
  Of dear Santa Claus.

Again, in his manhood's beginning,
  He sees himself thrown on the world,

13

And into the vortex of sinning
  By Pleasure's strong arms he is hurled.
He hears the sweet Christmas bells ringing,
  "Repent ye, repent ye, and pray";
But he joins with his comrades in singing
  A bacchanal lay.

Again he stands under the holly
  With a blushing face lifted to his
For love has been stronger than folly,
  And has turned him from vice unto bliss;
And the whole world is lit with new glory
  As the sweet vows are uttered again,
While the Christmas bells tell the old story
  Of peace unto men.

Again, with his little brood 'round him,
  He sits by the fair mother-wife;
He knows that the angels have crowned him
  With the truest, best riches of life;
And the hearts of the children, untroubled,
  Are filled with the gay Christmas-tide;
And the gifts for sweet Maudie are doubled,
  Tis her birthday, beside.

Again,—ah, dear Jesus, have pity—
  He finds in the chill, waning day,
That one has come home from the city—
  Frail Maudie, whom love led astray.
She lies with her babe on her bosom—
  Half-hid by the snow's fleecy spread;
A bud and a poor trampled blossom—
  And both are quite dead.

So fair and so fragile! just twenty—
  How mocking the bells sound to-night!

She starved in this great land of plenty,
  When she tried to grope back to the light.
Christ. are Thy disciples inhuman,
  Or only for men hast Thou died?
No mercy is shown to a woman
  Who once steps aside.

Again he leans over the shrouded
  Still form of the mother and wife;
Very lonely the way seems, and clouded,
  As he looks down the vista of life.
With the sweet Christmas chimes there is blended
  The knell for a life that is done,
And he knows that his joys are all ended
  And his waiting begun.

So long have the years been, so lonely,
  As he counts them by Christmases gone.
"I am homesick," he murmurs; "if only
  The Angel would lead the way on.
I am cold, in this chill winter weather;
  Why, Maudie, dear, where have you been?
And you, too, sweet wife—and together—
  O Christ, let me in"

The children ran in from the hallway,
  "Were you calling us, grandpa?" they said.
Then shrank, with that fear that comes alway
  When young eyes look their first on the dead.
The freedom so longed for is given.
  The children speak low and draw near:
"Dear grandpa keeps Christmas in Heaven
  With grandma, this year."

AFTER THE ENGAGEMENT

Well, Mabel, 'tis over and ended—
  The ball I wrote was to be;
And oh! it was perfectly splendid—
  If you could have been here to see.
I've a thousand things to write you
  That I know you are wanting to hear,
And one, that is sure to delight you—
  I am wearing Joe's diamond, my dear!

Yes, mamma is quite ecstatic
  That I am engaged to Joe;
She thinks I am rather erratic,
  And feared that I might say "No."
But, Mabel, I'm twenty-seven
  (Though nobody dreams it, dear),
And a fortune like Joe's isn't given
  To lay at one's feet each year.

You know my old fancy for Harry—
  Or, at least, I am certain you guessed
That it took all my sense not to marry
  And go with that fellow out west.
But that was my very first season—
  And Harry was poor as could be,
And mamma's good practical reason
  Took all the romance out of me.

She whisked me off over the ocean,
  And had me presented at court,

16

And got me all out of the notion
  That ranch life out west was my forte.
Of course I have never repented —
  I'm not such a goose of a thing;
But after I had consented
  To Joe — and he gave me the ring —

I felt such a queer sensation.
  I seemed to go into a trance,
Away from the music's pulsation,
  Away from the lights and the dance.
And the wind o'er the wild prairie
  Seemed blowing strong and free,
And it seemed not Joe, but Harry
  Who was standing there close to me.

And the funniest feverish feeling
  Went up from my feet to my head,
With little chills after it stealing —
  And my hands got as numb as the dead.
A moment, and then it was over:
  The diamond blazed up in my eyes,
And I saw in the face of my lover
  A questioning, strange surprise.

Maybe 'twas the scent of the flowers,
  That heavy with fragrance bloomed near,
But I didn't feel natural for hours;
  It was odd now, wasn't it, dear?
Write soon to your fortunate Clara,
  Who has carried the prize away,
And say you'll come on when I marry, —
  I think it will happen in May.

A HOLIDAY

The Wife

The house is like a garden,
  The children are the flowers,
The gardener should come methinks
  And walk among his bowers,
Oh! lock the door on worry
  And shut your cares away,
Not time of year, but love and cheer,
  Will make a holiday.

The Husband

Impossible! You women do not know
The toil it takes to make a business grow.
I cannot join you until very late,
So hurry home, nor let the dinner wait.

The Wife

The feast will be like Hamlet
  Without a Hamlet part:
The home is but a house, dear,
  Till you supply the heart.
The Xmas gift I long for
  You need not toil to buy;
Oh! give me back one thing I lack—
  The love-light in your eye.

18

The Husband

Of course I love you, and the children too
Be sensible, my dear, it is for you
I work so hard to make my business pay.
There, now, run home, enjoy your holiday.

The Wife (turning)

He does not mean to wound me,
  I know his heart is kind.
Alas! that man can love us
  And be so blind, so blind.
A little time for pleasure,
  A little time for play;
A word to prove the life of love
  And frighten Care away!
Tho' poor my lot in some small cot
  That were a holiday.

The Husband (musing)

She has not meant to wound me, nor to vex—
Zounds! but 'tis difficult to please the sex.
I've housed and gowned her like a very queen
Yet there she goes, with discontented mien.
I gave her diamonds only yesterday:
Some women are like that, do what you may.

FALSE

False! Good God, I am dreaming!
  No, no, it never can be—
You who are so true in seeming,
  You, false to your vows and me?
My wife and my fair boy's mother
  The star of my life—my queen—
To yield herself to another
  Like some light Magdalene!

Proofs! what are proofs—I defy them!
  They never can shake my trust;
If you look in my face and deny them
  I will trample them into the dust.
For whenever I read of the glory
  Of the realms of Paradise,
I sought for the truth of the story
  And found it in your sweet eyes.

Why, you are the shy young creature
  I wooed in her maiden grace;
There was purity in each feature,
  And my heaven I found in your face.
And, "not only married but mated,"
  I would say in my pride and joy;
And our hopes were all consummated
  When the angels gave us our boy.

Now you could not blot that beginning
  So beautiful, pure and true,

20

With a record of wicked sinning
  As a common woman might do.
Look up in your old frank fashion,
  With your smile so free from art;
And say that no guilty passion
  Has ever crept into your heart.

How pallid you are, and you tremble!
  You are hiding your face from view!
"Tho' a sinner, you cannot dissemble" —
  My God! then the tale is true?
True, and the sun above us
  Shines on in the summer skies?
And men say the angels love us,
  And that God is good and wise.

Yet he lets a wanton thing like you
  Ruin my home and my name!
Get out of my sight or I strike you
  Dead in your shameless shame!
No, no, I was wild, I was brutal;
  I would not take your life,
For the efforts of death would be futile
  To wipe out the sin of a wife.
Wife—why, that word has seemed sainted
  I uttered it like a prayer;
And now to think it is tainted—
  Christ! how much we can bear!

"Slay you!" my boy's stained mother—
  Nay, that would not punish, or save;
A soul that has outraged another
  Finds no sudden peace in the grave.
I will leave you here to remember
  The Eden that was your own,
While on toward my life's December
  I walk in the dark alone.

TWO SINNERS

There was a man, it was said one time,
Who went astray in his youthful prime.
Can the brain keep cool and the heart keep quiet
When the blood is a river that's running riot?
And boys will be boys, the old folks say,
And a man is the better who's had his day

The sinner reformed; and the preacher told
Of the prodigal son who came back to the fold.
And Christian people threw open the door,
With a warmer welcome than ever before.
Wealth and honour were his to command,
And a spotless woman gave him her hand.
And the world strewed their pathway with blossoms
abloom,
Crying, "God bless ladye, and God bless groom!"

There was a maiden who went astray,
In the golden dawn of her life's young day.
She had more passion and heart than head,
And she followed blindly where fond Love led.
And Love unchecked is a dangerous guide
To wander at will by a fair girl's side.

The woman repented and turned from sin,
But no door opened to let her in.
The preacher prayed that she might be forgiven,
But told her to look for mercy—in heaven.

22

For this is the law of the earth, we know:
That the woman is stoned, while the man may go.

A brave man wedded her after all,
But the world said, frowning, "We shall not call."

THE PHANTOM BALL

You remember the hall on the corner?
  To-night as I walked down street
I heard the sound of music,
  And the rhythmic beat and beat,
In time to the pulsing measure
  Of lightly tripping feet.

And I turned and entered the doorway—
  It was years since I had been there—
Years, and life seemed altered:
  Pleasure had changed to care.
But again I was hearing the music
  And watching the dancers fair.

And then, as I stood and listened,
  The music lost its glee;
And instead of the merry waltzers
  There were ghosts of the Used-to-be—
Ghosts of the pleasure-seekers
  Who once had danced with me.

Oh, 'twas a ghastly picture!
  Oh, 'twas a gruesome crowd!
Each bearing a skull on his shoulder,
  Each trailing a long white shroud,
As they whirled in the dance together,
  And the music shrieked aloud.

As they danced, their dry bones rattled
  Like shutters in a blast;
And they stared from eyeless sockets
  On me as they circled past;
And the music that kept them whirling
  Was a funeral dirge played fast.

Some of them wore their face-cloths,
  Others were rotted away.
Some had mould on their garments,
  And some seemed dead but a day.
Corpses all, but I knew them
  As friends, once blithe and gay.

Beauty and strength and manhood—
  And this was the end of it all:
Nothing but phantoms whirling
  In a ghastly skeleton ball.
But the music ceased—and they vanished,
  And I came away from the hall.

WORDS AND THOUGHTS

He said as he sat in her theatre box
Between the acts, "What beastly weather!
How like a parrot the lover talks—
And the lady is tame, and the villain stalks—
I hope they finally die together."

He thought—"You are fair as the dawn's first ray;
I know the angels keep guard above you.
And so I chatter of weather, and play,
While all the time I am mad to say,
I love you, love you, love you."

He said—"The season is almost run;
How glad we are, when the whirl is over!
For the toil of pleasure is more than its fun,
And what is it all, when all is done,
But the stick of a rocket that has descended?"

He thought—"Oh God! to be off somewhere
Afar with you, from this scene of fashion;
To know you were mine, and to have you care,
And to lose myself in the crimson snare
Of your lips, in a kiss of passion."

He said—"You are going abroad, no doubt,
This land of Liberty coldly scorning.
I too shall journey a bit about,

From Wall Street up by the L. Road out
To Harlem, and down each morning."

He thought—"It must follow on land or sea,
This pent-up, passionate, dumb devotion,
Till the cry of a rapture that may not be
Shall reach your heart from the heart of me
And stir you with strange emotion."

WANTED—A LITTLE GIRL

Where have they gone to—the little girls
With natural manners and natural curls;
Who love their dollies and like their toys,
And talk of something besides the boys?

Little old women in plenty I find,
Mature in manners and old of mind;
Little old flirts who talk of their "beaux,"
And vie with each other in stylish clothes.

Little old belles who, at nine and ten,
Are sick of pleasure and tired of men;
Weary of travel, of balls, of fun,
And find no new thing under the sun.

Once, in the beautiful long ago,
Some dear little children I used to know;
Girls who were merry as lambs at play,
And laughed and rollicked the livelong day.

They thought not at all of the "style" of their clothes,
They never imagined that boys were "beaux" —
"Other girls' brothers" and "mates" were they,
Splendid fellows to help them play.

Where have they gone to? If you see
One of them anywhere send her to me.

I would give a medal of purest gold
To one of those dear little girls of old,
With an innocent heart and an open smile,
Who knows not the meaning of "flirt" or "style."

THE SUICIDE

Vast was the wealth I carried in life's pack—
  Youth, health, ambition, hope and trust; but Time
  And Fate, those robbers fit for any crime,
Stole all, and left me but the empty sack.
Before me lay a long and lonely track
  Of darkling hills and barren steeps to climb;
  Behind me lay in shadows the sublime
Lost lands of Love's delight. Alack! Alack!

Unwearied, and with springing steps elate,
  I had conveyed my wealth along the road.
  The empty sack proved now a heavier load:
I was borne down beneath its worthless weight.
I stumbled on, and knocked at Death's dark gate.
  There was no answer. Stung by sorrow's goad
  I forced my way into that grim abode,
And laughed, and flung Life's empty sack to Fate.

Unknown and uninvited I passed in
  To that strange land that hangs between two goals,
  Round which a dark and solemn river rolls—
More dread its silence than the loud earth's din.
And now, where was the peace I hoped to win?
  Black-masted ships slid past me in great shoals,
  Their bloody decks thronged with mistaken souls.
(God punishes mistakes sometimes like sin.)

Not rest and not oblivion I found.
  My suffering self dwelt with me just the same;

But here no sleep was, and no sweet dreams came
To give me respite. Tyrant Death, uncrowned
By my own hand, still King of Terrors, frowned
   Upon my shuddering soul, that shrank in shame
   Before those eyes where sorrow blent with blame,
And those accusing lips that made no sound.

What gruesome shapes dawned on my startled sight
   What awful sighs broke on my listening ear!
   The anguish of the earth, augmented here
A thousand-fold, made one continuous night.
The sack I flung away in impious spite
   Hung yet upon me, filled, I saw in fear.
   With tears that rained from earth's adjacent sphere,
And turned to stones in falling from that height.

And close about me pressed a grieving throng,
   Each with his heavy sack, which bowed him so
   His face was hidden. One of these mourned: "Know
Who enters here but finds the way more long
To those fair realms where sounds the angels' song.
   There is no man-made exit out of woe;
   Ye cannot dash the locked door down and go
To claim thy rightful joy through paths of wrong."

He passed into the shadows dim and grey,
   And left me to pursue my path alone.
   With terror greater than I yet had known.
Hard on my soul the awful knowledge lay,
Death had not ended life nor found God's way;
   But, with my same sad sorrows still my own,
   Where by-roads led to by-roads, thistle-sown,
I had but wandered off and gone astray.

With earth still near enough to hear its sighs,
   With heaven afar and hell but just below,

Still on and on my lonely soul must go
Until I earn the right to Paradise.
We cannot force our way into God's skies,
  Nor rush into the rest we long to know;
  But patiently, with bleeding steps and slow
Toil on to where selfhood in Godhood dies.

"NOW I LAY ME"

When I pass from earth away,
Palsied though I be and grey,
May my spirit keep so young
That my failing, faltering tongue
Frames that prayer so dear to me,
Taught me at my mother's knee:
"Now I lay me down to sleep,"
(Passing to Eternal rest
On the loving parent breast)
"I pray the Lord my soul to keep;"
(From all danger safe and calm
In the hollow of His palm;)
"If I should die before I wake,"
(Drifting with a bated breath
Out of slumber into death,)
"I pray the Lord my soul to take."
(From the body's claim set free
Sheltered in the Great to be.)
Simple prayer of trust and truth.
Taught me in my early youth—
Let my soul its beauty keep
When I lay me down to sleep.

THE MESSENGER

She rose up in the early dawn,
  And white and silently she moved
About the house. Four men had gone
  To battle for the land they loved,
And she, the mother and the wife,
Waited for tidings from the strife.
How still the house seemed! and her tread
Was like the footsteps of the dead.

The long day passed, the dark night came;
  She had not seen a human face.
Some voice spoke suddenly her name.
  How loud it echoed in that place
Where, day by day, no sound was heard
But her own footsteps! "Bring you word,"
She cried to whom she could not see,
"Word from the battle-plain to me?"

A soldier entered at the door,
  And stood within the dim firelight:
"I bring you tidings of the four,"
  He said, "who left you for the fight."
"God bless you, friend," she cried; "speak on!
For I can bear it. One is gone?"
"Ay, one is gone!" he said. "Which one?"
"Dear lady, he, your eldest son."

A deathly pallor shot across
  Her withered face; she did not weep.

She said: "It is a grievous loss,
   But God gives His belovèd sleep.
What of the living—of the three?
And when can they come back to me?"
The soldier turned away his head:
"Lady, your husband, too, is dead."

She put her hand upon her brow;
   A wild, sharp pain was in her eyes.
"My husband! Oh, God, help me now!"
   The soldier heard her shuddering sighs.
The task was harder than he thought.
"Your youngest son, dear madam, fought
Close at his father's side; both fell
Dead, by the bursting of a shell."

She moved her lips and seemed to moan.
   Her face had paled to ashen grey:
"Then one is left me—one alone,"
   She said, "of four who marched away.
Oh, overruling, All-wise God,
How can I pass beneath Thy rod!"
The soldier walked across the floor,
Paused at the window, at the door,

Wiped the cold dew-drops from his cheek
   And sought the mourner's side again.
"Once more, dear lady, I must speak:
   Your last remaining son was slain
Just at the closing of the fight;
Twas he who sent me here to-night."
"God knows," the man said afterward,
"The fight itself was not so hard."

A SERVIAN LEGEND

Long, long ago, ere yet our race began,
When earth was empty, waiting still for man,
Before the breath of life to him was given
The angels fell into a strife in heaven.

At length one furious demon grasped the sun
And sped away as fast as he could run,
And with a ringing laugh of fiendish mirth,
He leaped the battlements and fell to earth.

Dark was it then in heaven, but light below;
For there the demon wandered to and fro,
Tilting aloft upon a slender pole
The orb of day—the pilfering old soul.

The angels wept and wailed; but through the dark
The Great Creator's voice cried sternly: "Hark!
Who will restore to me the orb of Light,
Him will I honour in all heaven's sight."

Then over the battlements there dropped another.
(A shrewder angel well there could not be.)
Quoth he: "Behold my love for thee, my brother,
For I have left all heaven to stay with thee.

"Thy loneliness and wanderings I will share,
Thy heavy burden I will help thee bear."

"Well said," the demon answered, "and well done,
But I'll not tax you with this heavy sun.

"Your company will cheer me, it is true,
And I could never think of burdening you."
Idly they wandered onward, side by side,
Till, by and by, they neared a silvery tide.

"Let's bathe," the angel suddenly suggested.
"Agreed," the demon answered. "I'll go last,
Because I needs must leave quite unmolested
This tiresome sun, which I will now make fast.

He set the pole well in the sandy turf,
And called a jackdaw near to watch the place.
Meanwhile the angel paddled in the surf,
And playfully dared his brother to a race.

They swam around together for a while,
The demon always keeping near his prize,
Till presently the angel, with a smile,
Proposed a healthful diving exercise.

The demon hesitated. "But," thought he,
"The jackdaw will inform me with a cry
If this good brother tries deceiving me;
I will not be outdone by him—not I!"

Down, down they went. The angel in a trice
Rose up again, and swift to shore he sped.
The jackdaw shrieked, but lo! a mile of ice
The demon found had frozen o'er his head.

He swore an oath, and gathered all his force,
And broke the ice, to see the sun, of course,

Held firmly in the radiant angel's hand,
Who sailed away toward the heavenly land.

He gave pursuit. Wrath lent speed to his chase;
All heaven leaned down to watch the exciting race.
On, on they came, and still the Evil One
Gained on the angel burdened with the sun.

With bated breath and faces white as ghosts,
Over the walls leaned heaven's affrighted hosts.
Up, up, still up, the angel almost spent,
Threw one foot forward o'er the battlement.

The demon seized the other with a shout;
So fierce his clutch he pulled the bottom out,
As the good angel, fainting, laid the sun
Down by the throne of God, who cried: "Well done!
Thy great misfortune shall be made divine:
Man will I create with a foot like thine!"

PEEK-A-BOO

The cunningest thing that a baby can do
Is the very first time it plays peek-a-boo;

When it hides its pink little face in its hands,
And crows, and shows that it understands

What nurse, and mamma and papa, too,
Mean when they hide and cry, "Peek a-boo, peek-a-boo."

Oh, what a wonderful thing it is,
When they find that baby can play like this!

And every one listens, and thinks it true
That baby's gurgle means "Peek-a-boo, peek-a-boo";

And over and over the changes are rung
On the marvellous infant who talks so young.

I wonder if any one ever knew
A baby that never played peek-a-boo, peek-a-boo.

'Tis old as the hills are. I believe
Cain was taught it by Mother Eve;

For Cain was an innocent baby, too,
And I am sure he played peek-a-boo, peek-a-boo.

And the whole world full of the children of men,
Have all of them played that game since then.

Kings and princes and beggars, too,
Every one has played peek-a-boo, peek-a-boo.

Thief and robber and ruffian bold,
The crazy tramp and the drunkard old,

All have been babies who laughed and knew
How to hide, and play peek-a-boo, peek-a-boo.

THE FALLING OF THRONES

Above the din of commerce, above the clamour and rattle
  Of labour disputing with riches, of Anarchists' threats and groans,
Above the hurry and hustle and roar of that bloodless battle,
  Where men are fighting for riches, I hear the falling of thrones.

I see no savage host, I hear no martial drumming,
  But down in the dust at our feet lie the useless crowns of kings;
And the mighty spirit of Progress is steadily coming, coming,
  And the flag of one republic abroad to the world he flings.

The Universal Republic, where worth, not birth, is royal;
  Where the lowliest born may climb on a self-made ladder to fame;
Where the highest and proudest born, if he be not true and loyal,
  Shall find no masking title to cover and gild his shame.

Not with the bellow of guns and not with sabres whetting,
  But with growing minds of men is waged this swordless fray;
While over the dim horizon the sun of royalty, setting,
  Lights, with a dying splendour, the humblest toiler's way.

HER LAST LETTER

Sitting alone by the window,
  Watching the moonlit street,
Bending my head to listen
  To the well-known sound of your feet,
I have been wondering, darling,
  How I can bear the pain,
When I watch, with sighs and tear-wet eyes,
  And wait for your coming in vain.

For I know that a day approaches
  When your heart will tire of me;
When by door and gate I may watch and wait
  For a form I shall not see;
When the love that is now my heaven,
  The kisses that make my life,
You will bestow on another,
  And that other will be—your wife.

You will grow weary of sinning
  (Though you do not call it so),
You will long for a love that is purer
  Than the love that we two know.
God knows I have loved you dearly,
  With a passion strong as true;
But you will grow tired and leave me,
  Though I gave up all for you.

I was as pure as the morning
  When I first looked on your face;

I knew I never could reach you
    In your high, exalted place.
But I looked and loved and worshipped
    As a flower might worship a star,
And your eyes shone down upon me,
    And you seemed so far—so far.

And then? Well, then, you loved me,
    Loved me with all your heart;
But we could not stand at the altar—
    We were so far apart.
If a star should wed with a flower
    The star must drop from the sky,
Or the flower in trying to reach it
    Would droop on its stalk and die.

But you said that you loved me, darling,
    And swore by the heavens above
That the Lord and all of His angels
    Would sanction and bless our love.
And I? I was weak, not wicked.
    My love was as pure as true,
And sin itself seemed a virtue
    If only shared by you.

We have been happy together,
    Though under the cloud of sin,
But I know that the day approaches
    When my chastening must begin.
You have been faithful and tender,
    But you will not always be,
But I think I had better leave you
    While your thoughts are kind of me.

I know my beauty is fading—
    Sin furrows the fairest brow—

And I know that your heart will weary
  Of the face you smile on now.
You will take a bride to your bosom
  After you turn from me;
You will sit with your wife in the moonlight,
  And bold her babe on your knee.

O God! I never could bear it;
  It would madden my brain, I know;
And so while you love me dearly
  I think I had better go.
It is sweeter to feel, my darling—
  To know as I fall asleep—
That some one will mourn me and miss me,
  That some one is left to weep,

Than to die as I should in the future,
  To drop in the street some day,
Unknown, unwept, and forgotten
  After you cast me away.
Perhaps the blood of the Saviour
  Can wash my garments clean;
Perchance I may drink of the waters
  That flow through pastures green.

Perchance we may meet in heaven,
  And walk in the streets above,
With nothing to grieve us or part us
  Since our sinning was all through love
God says, "Love one another,"
  And down to the depths of hell
Will He send the soul of a woman
  Because she loved—and fell?

* * *

And so in the moonlight he found her,
　Or found her beautiful clay,
Lifeless and pallid as marble,
　For the spirit had flown away.
The farewell words she had written
　She held to her cold, white breast,
And the buried blade of a dagger
　Told how she had gone to rest.

THE PRINCESS'S FINGER-NAIL

A TALE OF NONSENSE LAND

All through the Castle of High-bred Ease,
Where the chief employment was do-as-you-please,
Spread consternation and wild despair.
The queen was wringing her hands and hair;
The maids of honour were sad and solemn;
The pages looked blank as they stood in column;
The court-jester blubbered, "Boo-hoo, boo-hoo"
The cook in the kitchen dropped tears in the stew
And all through the castle went sob and wail,
For the princess had broken her finger-nail:
The beautiful Princess Red-as-a-Rose,
Bride-elect of the Lord High-Nose,
Broken her finger-nail down to the quick—
No wonder the queen and her court were sick.
Never sorrow so dread before
Had dared to enter that castle door.
Oh! what would my Lord His-High-Nose say
When she took off her glove on her wedding-day?
The fairest princess in Nonsense Land,
With a broken finger-nail on her hand!
'Twas a terrible, terrible accident,
And they called a meeting of parliament;
And never before that royal Court
Had come such question of grave import

As "How could you hurry a nail to grow?"
And the skill of the kingdom was called to show.
They sent for Monsieur File-'em-off;
He smoothed down the corners so ragged and rough.
They sent for Madame la Diamond-Dust,
Who lived on the fingers of upper-crust;
They sent for Professor de Chamois-Skin,
Who took her powder and rubbed it in;
They sent for the pudgy nurse Fat-on-the-Bone
To bathe her finger in eau-de-Cologne;
And they called the court surgeon, Monsieur Red-Tape,
To hear what he thought of the new nail's shape,
Over the kingdom the telegrams flew
Which told how the finger-nail thrived and grew;
And all through the realm of Nonsense Land
They offered up prayers for the princess's hand.
At length the glad tidings were heard with a shout
What the princess's finger-nail had grown out:
Pointed and polished and pink and clean,
Befitting the hand of a some-day queen.
Salutes were fired all over the land
By the home-guard battery pop-gun band;
And great was the joy of my Lord High-Nose,
Who straightway ordered his wedding clothes,
And paid his tailor, Don Wait-for-aye,
Who died of amazement the self-same day.
My lord by a jury was judged insane;
For they said—and the truth of the saying was plain—
That a lord of such very high pedigree
Would never be paying his bills, you see,
Unless he was out of his head; and so
They locked him up without more ado.
And the beautiful Princess Red-as-a-Rose
Pined for her lover, my Lord High-Nose,
Till she entered a convent and took the veil—
And this is the end of my nonsense tale.

A BABY IN THE HOUSE

I knew that a baby was hid in the house;
   Though I saw no cradle and heard no cry,
But the husband went tiptoeing round like a mouse,
   And the good wife was humming a soft lullaby;
And there was a look on the face of that mother
That I knew could mean only one thing, and no other.

"The mother," I said to myself; for I knew
   That the woman before me was certainly that,
For there lay in the corner a tiny cloth shoe,
   And I saw on the stand such a wee little hat;
And the beard of the husband said plain as could be,
"Two fat, chubby hands have been tugging at me."

And he took from his pocket a gay picture-book,
   And a dog that would bark if you pulled on a string;
And the wife laid them up with such a pleased look;
   And I said to myself, "There is no other thing
But a babe that could bring about all this, and so
That one is in hiding here somewhere, I know."

I stayed but a moment, and saw nothing more,
   And heard not a sound, yet I knew I was right;
What else could the shoe mean that lay on the floor,
   The book and the toy, and the faces so bright?
And what made the husband as still as a mouse?
I am sure, very sure, there's a babe in that house.

THE FOOLISH ELM

The bold young Autumn came riding along
  One day where an elm-tree grew.
"You are fair," he said, as she bent down her head,
  "Too fair for your robe's dull hue.
You are far too young for a garb so old;
  Your beauty needs colour and sheen.
Oh, I would clothe you in scarlet and gold
  Befitting the grace of a queen.

"For one little kiss on your lips, sweet elm,
  For one little kiss, no more,
I would give you, I swear, a robe more fair
  Than ever a princess wore.
One little kiss on those lips, my pet,
  And lo! you shall stand, I say,
Queen of the forest, and, better yet,
  Queen of my heart alway."

She tossed her head, but he took the kiss—
  'Tis the way of lovers bold—
And a gorgeous dress for that sweet caress
  He gave ere the morning was old.
For a week and a day she ruled a queen
  In beauty and splendid attire;
For a week and a day she was loved, I ween,
  With the love that is born of desire.

Then bold-eyed Autumn went on his way
  In search of a tree more fair;

And mob-winds tattered her garments and scattered
　Her finery here and there.
Poor and faded and ragged and cold
　She rocked in her wild distress,
And longed for the dull green gown she had sold
　For her fickle lover's caress.

And the days went by and Winter came,
　And his tyrannous tempests beat
On the shivering tree, whose robes of flame
　He had trampled under his feet.
I saw her reach up to the mocking skies
　Her poor arms, bare and thin;
Ah, well-a-day! it is ever the way
　With a woman who trades with sin.

ROBIN'S MISTAKE

What do you think Red Robin
Found by a mow of hay?
Why, a flask brimful of liquor,
That the mowers brought that day
To slake their thirst in the hayfield.
And Robin he shook his head:
"Now I wonder what they call it,
And how it tastes?" he said.

"I have seen the mowers drink it—
Why isn't it good for me?
So I'll just draw out the stopper
And get at the stuff, and see!"
But alas! for the curious Robin,
One draught, and he burned his throat
From his bill to his poor crop's lining,
And he could not utter a note.

And his head grew light and dizzy,
And he staggered left and right,
Tipped over the flask of brandy,
And spilled it, every mite.
But after awhile he sobered,
And quietly flew away,
And he never has tasted liquor,
Or touched it, since that day.

But I heard him say to his kindred,
In the course of a friendly chat,

"These men think they are above us,
Yet they drink such stuff as that!
Oh, the poor degraded creatures!
I am glad I am only a bird!"
Then he flew up over the meadow,
And that was all I heard.

NEW YEAR RESOLVE

As the dead year is clasped by a dead December,
   So let your dead sins with your dead days lie.
A new life is yours and a new hope. Remember
   We build our own ladders to climb to the sky.

Stand out in the sunlight of promise, forgetting
   Whatever the past held of sorrow and wrong.
We waste half our strength in a useless regretting;
   We sit by old tombs in the dark too long.

Have you missed in your aim? Well, the mark is still
shining.
   Did you faint in the race? Well, take breath for the next.
Did the clouds drive you back? But see yonder their lining.
   Were you tempted and fell? Let it serve for a text.

As each year hurries by, let it join that procession
   Of skeleton shapes that march down to the past,
While you take your place in the line of progression,
   With your eyes to the heavens, your face to the blast.

I tell you the future can hold no terrors
   For any sad soul while the stars revolve,
If he will stand firm on the grave of his errors,
   And instead of regretting—resolve, resolve!

It is never too late to begin rebuilding,
   Though all into ruins your life seems hurled;

For see! how the light of the New Year is gilding
The wan, worn face of the bruised old world.

WHAT WE WANT

All hail the dawn of a new day breaking,
When a strong-armed nation shall take away
The weary burdens from backs that are aching
With maximum labour and minimum pay;
When no man is honoured who hoards his millions;
When no man feasts on another's toil;
And God's poor suffering, striving billions
Shall share His riches of sun and soil.

There is gold for all in the earth's broad bosom,
There is food for all in the land's great store;
Enough is provided if rightly divided;
Let each man take what he needs—no more.
Shame on the miser with unused riches,
Who robs the toiler to swell his hoard,
Who beats down the wage of the digger of ditches,
And steals the bread from the poor man's board.

Shame on the owner of mines whose cruel
And selfish measures have brought him wealth,
While the ragged wretches who dig his fuel
Are robbed of comfort and hope and health.
Shame on the ruler who rides in his carriage
Bought with the labour of half-paid men—
Men who are shut out of home and marriage
And are herded like sheep in a hovel-pen.

Let the clarion voice of the nation wake him
To broader vision and fairer play;

Or let the hand of a just law shake him
Till his ill-gained dollars shall roll away.
Let no man dwell under a mountain of plunder,
Let no man suffer with want and cold;
We want right living, not mere alms-giving;
We want just dividing of labour and gold.

BREAKING THE DAY IN TWO

When from dawn till noon seems one long day,
  And from noon till night another,
Oh, then should a little boy come from play,
  And creep into the arms of his mother.
Snugly creep and fall asleep,
  Oh, come, my baby, do;
Creep into my lap, and with a nap
  We'll break the day in two.

When the shadows slant for afternoon,
  When the midday meal is over,
When the winds have sung themselves into a swoon,
  And the bees drone in the clover,
Then hie to me, hie, for a lullaby—
  Come, my baby, do;
Creep into my lap, and with a nap
  We'll break the day in two.

We'll break it in two with a crooning song,
  With a soft and soothing number;
For the day has no right to be so long
  And keep my baby from slumber.
Then rock-a-by, rock, may white dreams flock
  Like angels over you;
Baby's gone, and the deed is done,
  We've broken the day in two.

THE RAPE OF THE MIST

High o'er the clouds a Sunbeam shone,
  And far down under him,
With a subtle grace that was all her own,
  The Mist gleamed, fair and dim.

He looked at her with his burning eyes
  And longed to fall at her feet;
Of all sweet things there under the skies,
  He thought her the thing most sweet.

He had wooed oft, as a Sunbeam may,
  Wave, and blossom, and flower;
But never before had he felt the sway
  Of a great love's mighty power.

Tall cloud-mountains and vast space-seas,
  Wind, and tempest, and fire—
What are obstacles such as these
  To a heart that is filled with desire?

Boldly he trod over cloud and star,
  Boldly he swam through space,
She caught the glow of his eyes afar
  And veiled her delicate face.

He was so strong and he was so bright,
  And his breath was a breath of flame;

The Mist grew pale with a vague, strange fright,
   As fond, yet fierce, he came.

Close to his heart she was clasped and kissed;
   She swooned in love's alarms,
And dead lay the beautiful pale-faced Mist
   In the Sunbeam's passionate arms.

THE TWO GLASSES

There sat two glasses, filled to the brim,
On a rich man's table, rim to rim.
One was ruddy and red as blood,
And one was as clear as the crystal flood.

Said the glass of wine to his paler brother:
"Let us tell tales of the past to each other.
I can tell of banquet, and revel, and mirth,
Where I was king, for I ruled in might;
And the proudest and grandest souls on earth
Fell under my touch, as though struck with blight.
From the heads of kings I have torn the crown;
From the heights of fame I have hurled men down;
I have blasted many an honoured name;
I have taken virtue and given shame;
I have tempted the youth, with a sip, a taste,
That has made his future a barren waste.
Far greater than any king am I,
Or than any army under the sky.
I have made the arm of the driver fail,
And sent the train from its iron rail.
I have made good ships go down at sea,
And the shrieks of the lost were sweet to me.
Fame, strength, wealth, genius, before me fall,
And my might and power are over all.
Ho! ho! pale brother," laughed the wine,
"Can you boast of deeds as great as mine?"

Said the glass of water: "I cannot boast
Of a king dethroned or a murdered host;
But I can tell of hearts that were sad,
By my crystal drops made light and glad;
Of thirsts I have quenched, and brows I have laved;
Of hands I have cooled and souls I have saved.
I have leaped through the valley and dashed down the
mountain;
Slept in the sunshine and dripped from the fountain.
I have burst my cloud-fetters and dropped from the sky,
And everywhere gladdened the landscape and eye.
I have eased the hot forehead of fever and pain;
I have made the parched meadows grow fertile with grain;
I can tell of the powerful wheel o' the mill,
That ground out the flour and turned at my will;
I can tell of manhood, debased by you,
That I have uplifted and crowned anew.
I cheer, I help, I strengthen and aid,
I gladden the heart of man and maid;
I set the chained wine-captive free,
And all are better for knowing me."

These are the tales they told each other,
The glass of wine and its paler brother,
As they sat together, filled to the brim,
On the rich man's table, rim to rim.

THE MANIAC

I saw them sitting in the shade;
  The long green vines hung over,
But could not hide the gold-haired maid
  And Earl, my dark-eyed lover.
His arm was clasped so close, so close,
  Her eyes were softly lifted,
While his eyes drank the cheek of rose
  And breasts like snowflakes drifted.

A strange noise sounded in my brain;
  I was a guest unbidden.
I stole away, but came again
  With two knives snugly hidden.
I stood behind them. Close they kissed,
  While eye to eye was speaking;
I aimed my steels, and neither missed
  The heart I sent it seeking.

There were two death-shrieks mingled so
  It seemed like one voice crying,
I laughed—it was such bliss, you know,
  To hear and see them dying.
I laughed and shouted while I stood
  Above the lovers, gazing
Upon the trickling rills of blood
  And frightened eyes fast glazing.

It was such joy to see the rose
  Fade from her cheek for ever;

To know the lips he kissed so close
  Could answer never, never.
To see his arm grow stark and cold,
  And know it could not hold her;
To know that while the world grew old
  His eyes could not behold her.

A crowd of people thronged about,
  Brought thither by my laughter;
I gave one last triumphant shout—
  Then darkness followed after.
That was a thousand years ago;
  Each hour I live it over,
For there, just out of reach, you know,
  She lies, with Earl, my lover.

They lie there, staring, staring so
  With great, glazed eyes to taunt me.
Will no one bury them down low,
  Where they shall cease to haunt me?
He kissed her lips, not mine; the flowers
  And vines hung all about them.
Sometimes I sit and laugh for hours
  To think just how I found them.

And then I sometimes stand and shriek
  In agony of terror:
I see the red warm in her cheek,
  Then laugh loud at my error.
My cheek was all too pale, he thought;
  He deemed hers far the brightest.
Ha! but my dagger touched a spot
  That made her face the whitest!

But oh! the days seem very long,
  Without my Earl, my lover;

And something in my head seems wrong
   The more I think it over.
Ah! look—she is not dead—look there!
   She's standing close beside me!
Her eyes are open—how they stare!
   Oh, hide me! hide me! hide me!

WHAT IS FLIRTATION?

What is flirtation? Really,
  How can I tell you that?
But when she smiles I see its wiles,
  And when he lifts his hat.

'Tis walking in the moonlight,
  'Tis buttoning on a glove,
'Tis lips that speak of plays next week,
  While eyes are talking love.

'Tis meeting in the ball-room,
  'Tis whirling in the dance;
'Tis something hid beneath the lid
  More than a simple glance.

'Tis lingering in the hallway,
  'Tis sitting on the stair,
'Tis bearded lips on finger-tips,
  If mamma isn't there.

'Tis tucking in the carriage,
  'Tis asking for a call;
'Tis long good-nights in tender lights,
  And that is—no, not all!

'Tis parting when it's over,
  And one goes home to sleep;
Best joys must end, tra la, my friend,
  But one goes home to weep!

HUSBAND AND WIFE

Reach out your arms, and hold me close and fast,
Tell me you have no memories of your past
That mar this love of ours, so great, so vast.

Some truths are cheapened when too oft averred—
Does not the deed speak louder than the word?
(Dear Christ! that old dream woke again and stirred.)

As you love me, you never loved before?
Though oft you say it—say it yet once more;
My heart is jealous of those days of yore.

Sweet wife, dear comrade, mother of my child,
My life is yours, by memory undefiled.
(It stirs again, that passion brief and wild.)

You never knew such happy hours as this,
We two alone, our hearts surcharged with bliss,
Nor other kisses sweet as my own kiss?

I was the thirsty field, long parched with drouth,
You were the warm rain blowing from the South.
(But oh! the crimson madness of her mouth.)

You would not, if you could, go down life's track
For just one little moment, and bring back
Some vanished raptures that you miss or lack?

66

I am content. You are my life, my all.
(One burning hour, but one, could I recall.
God! how men lie, when driven to the wall!)

HOW DOES LOVE SPEAK?

How does Love speak?
In the faint flush upon the tell-tale cheek,
And in the pallor that succeeds it; by
The quivering lid of an averted eye—
The smile that proves the parent of a sigh:
    Thus doth Love speak.

How does Love speak?
By the uneven heart-throbs, and the freak
Of bounding pulses that stand still and ache
While new emotions, like strange barges, make
Along vein-channels their disturbing course,
Still as the dawn, and with the dawn's swift force:
    Thus doth Love speak.

How does Love speak?
In the avoidance of that which we seek
The sudden silence and reserve when near;
The eye that glistens with an unshed tear;
The joy that seems the counterpart of fear,
As the alarmèd heart leads in the breast,
And knows, and names, and greets its godlike guest:
    Thus doth Love speak.

How does Love speak?
In the proud spirit suddenly grown meek,
The haughty heart grown humble; in the tender

And unnamed light that floods the world with splendour;
In the resemblance which the fond eyes trace
In all fair things to one belovèd face;
In the shy touch of hands that thrill and tremble;
In looks and lips that can no more dissemble:
    Thus doth Love speak.

    How does Love speak?
In wild words that uttered seem so weak
They shrink ashamed to silence; in the fire
Glance strikes with glance, swift flashing high and higher,
Like lightnings that precede the mighty storm
In the deep, soulful stillness; in the warm,
Impassioned tide that sweeps thro' throbbing veins,
Between the shores of keen delights and pains;
In the embrace where madness melts in bliss,
And in the convulsive rapture of a kiss:
    Thus doth Love speak.

REINCARNATION

He slept as weary toilers do,
   She gazed up at the moon.
He stirred and said, "Wife, come to bed";
   She answered, "Soon, full soon."
(Oh! that strange mystery of the dead moon's face.)

Her cheek was wan, her wistful mouth
   Was lifted like a cup,
The moonful night dripped liquid light:
   She seemed to quaff it up.
(Oh! that unburied corpse that lies in space.)

Her life had held but drudgery —
   She spelled her Bible thro';
Of books and lore she knew no more
   Than little children do.
(Oh! the weird wonder of that pallid sphere.)

Her youth had been a loveless waste,
   Starred by no holiday.
And she had wed for roof, and bread;
   She gave her work in pay.
(Oh! the moon-memories, vague and strange and dear.)

She drank the night's insidious wine,
   And saw another scene:
A stately room — rare flowers in bloom,

Herself in silken sheen.
(Oh! vast the chambers of the moon, and wide.)

A step drew near, a curtain stirred;
   She shook with sweet alarms.
Oh! splendid face; oh! manly grace;
   Oh! strong impassioned arms.
(Oh! silent moon, what secrets do you hide!)

The warm red lips of thirsting love
   On cheek and brow were pressed;
As the bees know where honeys grow,
   They sought her mouth, her breast.
(Oh! the dead moon holds many a dead delight.)

The speaker stirred and gruffly spake,
   "Come, wife, where have you been?"
She whispered low, "Dear God, I go—
   But 'tis the seventh sin."
(Oh! the sad secrets of that orb of white.)

AS YOU GO THROUGH LIFE

Don't look for the flaws as you go through life;
  And even when you find them,
It is wise and kind to be somewhat blind
  And look for the virtue behind them.
For the cloudiest night has a hint of light
  Somewhere in its shadows hiding;
It is better by far to hunt for a star,
  Than the spots on the sun abiding.

The current of life runs ever away
  To the bosom of God's great ocean.
Don't set your force 'gainst the river's course
  And think to alter its motion.
Don't waste a curse on the universe—
  Remember it lived before you.
Don't butt at the storm with your puny form,
  But bend and let it go o'er you.

The world will never adjust itself
  To suit your whims to the letter.
Some things must go wrong your whole life long,
  And the sooner you know it the better.
It is folly to fight with the Infinite,
  And go under at last in the wrestle;
The wiser man shapes into God's plan
  As water shapes into a vessel.

HOW SALVATOR WON

The gate was thrown open, I rode out alone,
More proud than a monarch who sits on a throne.
I am but a jockey, yet shout upon shout
Went up from the people who watched me ride out;
And the cheers that rang forth from that warm-hearted
crowd,
Were as earnest as those to which monarch e'er bowed.

My heart thrilled with pleasure so keen it was pain
As I patted my Salvator's soft silken mane;
And a sweet shiver shot from his hide to my hand
As we passed by the multitude down to the stand.

The great waves of cheering came billowing back,
As the hoofs of brave Tenny rang swift down the track;
And he stood there beside us, all bone and all muscle,
Our noble opponent, well trained for the tussle
That waited us there on the smooth, shining course.
My Salvator, fair to the lovers of horse,
As a beautiful woman is fair to man's sight—
Pure type of the thoroughbred, clean-limbed and bright,—
Stood taking the plaudits as only his due,
And nothing at all unexpected or new.

And then, there before us the bright flag is spread,
There's a roar from the grand stand, and Tenny's ahead;
At the sound of the voices that shouted "a go!"

He sprang like an arrow shot straight from the bow.
I tighten the reins on Prince Charlie's great son—
He is off like a rocket, the race is begun.
Half-way down the furlong, their heads are together,
Scarce room 'twixt their noses to wedge in a feather;
Past grand stand, and judges, in neck-to-neck strife,
Ah, Salvator, boy! 'tis the race of your life.
I press my knees closer, I coax him, I urge,
I feel him go out with a leap and a surge;
I see him creep on, inch by inch, stride by stride,
While backward, still backward, falls Tenny beside.
We are nearing the turn, the first quarter is past—
'Twixt leader and chaser the daylight is cast.
The distance elongates, still Tenny sweeps on,
As graceful and free-limbed and swift as a fawn;
His awkwardness vanished, his muscles all strained—
A noble opponent, well born and well trained.
I glanced o'er my shoulder, ha! Tenny, the cost
Of that one's second flagging, will be—the race lost.
One second's weak yielding of courage and strength,
And the daylight between us has doubled its length.

The first mile is covered, the race is mine—no!
For the blue blood of Tenny responds to a blow.
He shoots through the air like a ball from a gun,
And the two lengths between us are shortened to one,
My heart is contracted, my throat feels a lump,
For Tenny's long neck is at Salvator's rump;
And now with new courage grown bolder and bolder,
I see him, once more running shoulder to shoulder.
With knees, hands, and body I press my grand steed
I urge him, I coax him, I pray him to heed!
Oh, Salvator! Salvator! list to my calls,
For the blow of my whip will hurt both if it falls.
There's a roar from the crowd like the ocean in storm
As close to my saddle leaps Tenny's great form:

One more mighty plunge, and with knee, limb, and hand,
I lift my horse first by a nose past the stand.
We are under the string now—the great race is done,
And Salvator, Salvator, Salvator won!
Cheer, hoar-headed patriarchs; cheer loud, I say.
'Tis the race of a century witnessed to-day!
Though ye live twice the space that's allotted to men,
Ye never will see such a grand race again.
Let the shouts of the populace roar like the surf
For Salvator, Salvator, king of the turf!
He has broken the record of thirteen long years;
He has won the first place in a vast line of peers.
'Twas a neck-to-neck contest, a grand, honest race,
And even his enemies grant him his place.
Down into the dust let old records be hurled,
And hang out 2.05 in the gaze of the world.

THE WATCHER

"I think I hear the sound of horses feet
  Beating upon the gravelled avenue.
Go to the window that looks on the street,
  He would not let me die alone, I knew."
Back to the couch the patient watcher passed,
And said: "It is the wailing of the blast."

She turned upon her couch and, seeming, slept,
  The long, dark lashes shadowing her cheek;
And on and on the weary moments crept,
  When suddenly the watcher heard her speak:
"I think I hear the sound of horses' hoofs—"
And answered, "'Tis the rain upon the roofs."

Unbroken silence, quiet, deep, profound.
  The restless sleeper turns: "How dark, how late!
What is it that I hear—a trampling sound?
  I think there is a horseman at the gate."
The watcher turns away her eyes tear-blind:
"It is the shutter beating in the wind."

The dread hours passed; the patient clock ticked on;
  The weary watcher moved not from her place.
The grey dim shadows of the early dawn
  Caught sudden glory from the sleeper's face.
"He comes! my love! I knew he would!" she cried;
And, smiling sweetly in her slumbers, died.

HOW WILL IT BE?

How will it be when one of us alone
  Goes on that strange last journey of the soul?
That certain search for an uncertain goal,
  That voyage on which no comradeship is known?
Will our dear sea sing with the old sweet tone,
  Though one sits stricken where its billows roll?
Will space be dumb, or from the mystic pole
  Will spirit-messages be backward blown?
When our united lives are wrenched apart,
  And day no more means fond companionship,
When fervent night, and lovely languorous dawn,
  Are only memories to one sad heart,
And but in dreams love-kisses burn the lip,—
  Dear God, how can this same fair world move on?

MEMORY'S RIVER

In Nature's bright blossoms not always reposes
  That strange subtle essence more rare than their bloom,
Which lies in the hearts of carnations and roses,
  That unexplained something by men called perfume.
Though modest the flower, yet great is its power
  And pregnant with meaning each pistil and leaf,
If only it hides there, if only abides there,
  The fragrance suggestive of love, joy, and grief.

Not always the air that a master composes
  Can stir human heart-strings with pleasure or pain.
But strange, subtle chords, like the scent of the roses,
  Breathe out of some measures, though simple the strain.
And lo! when you hear them, you love them and fear them,
  You tremble with anguish, you thrill with delight,
For back of them slumber old dreams without number,
  And faces long vanished peer out into sight.

Those dear foolish days when the earth seemed all beauty,
  Before you had knowledge enough to be sad;
When youth held no higher ideal of duty
  Than just to lilt on through the world and be glad.
On harmony's river they seemed to afloat hither
  With all the sweet fancies that hung round that time—
Life's burdens and troubles turn into air-bubbles
  And break on the music's swift current of rhyme.

Fair Folly comes back with her spell while you listen
  And points to the paths where she led you of old.

You gaze on past sunsets, you see dead stars glisten,
     You bathe in life's glory, you swoon in death's cold.
All pains and all pleasures surge up through those measures,
     Your heart is wrenched open with earthquakes of sound;
From ashes and embers rise Junes and Decembers,
     Lost islands in fathoms of feeling refound.

Some airs are like outlets of memory's oceans,
     They rise in the past and flow into the heart;
And down them float shipwrecks of mighty emotions,
     All sea-soaked and storm-tossed and drifting apart:
Their fair timbers battered, their lordly sails tattered,
     Their skeleton crew of dead days on their decks;
Then a crash of chords blending, a crisis, an ending—
     The music is over, and vanished the wrecks.

LOVE'S WAY

Love gives us copious potions of delight,
   Of pain and ecstasy, and peace and care;
Love leads us upward, to the mountain height,
   And, like an angel, stands beside us there;
Then thrusts us, demon-like, in some abyss:
   Where, in the darkness of despair, we grope,
Till, suddenly, Love greets us with a kiss
   And guides us back to flowery fields of hope.

Love makes all wisdom seem but poorest folly,
   And yet the simplest mind with Love grows wise,
The gayest heart he teaches melancholy,
   Yet glorifies the erstwhile brooding eyes.
Love lives on change, and yet at change Love mocks,
   For Love's whole life is one great paradox.

A MAN'S LAST LOVE

Like the tenth wave, that offers to the shore
Accumulated opulence and force,
So does my heart, which thought it loved of yore,
   Carry increasing passion down the course
Of time to proffer thee.
        Oh! not the faint
   First ripple of the sea should be its pride,
But the great climax of its unrestraint,
   Which culminates in one commanding tide.

The lesser billows of each crude emotion
   Break on life's strand, recede, and then unite
With love's large sea; and to some late devotion
   Unrecognised, they bring their lost delight.
So all the vanished fancies of my past
Live yet in this one passion, grand and vast.

THE LADY AND THE DAME

So thou hast the art, good dame, thou swearest,
  To keep Time's perishing touch at bay
From the roseate splendour of the cheek so tender,
  And the silver threads from the gold away;
And the tell-tale years that have hurried by us
  Shall tiptoe back, and, with kind good-will,
They shall take their traces from off our faces,
  If we will trust to thy magic skill.

Thou speakest fairly; but if I listen
  And buy thy secret and prove its truth,
Hast thou the potion and magic lotion
  To give me also the heart of youth?
With the cheek of rose and the eye of beauty,
  And the lustrous locks of life's lost prime,
Wilt thou bring thronging each hope and longing
  That made the glory of that dead Time?

When the sap in the trees sets young buds bursting,
  And the song of the birds fills the air like spray,
Will rivers of feeling come once more stealing
  From the beautiful hills of the far-away?
Wilt thou demolish the tower of reason
  And fling for ever down into the dust
The caution Time brought me, the lessons life taught me,
  And put in their places my old sweet trust?

If Time's footprint from my brow is driven,
  Canst thou, too, take with thy subtle powers

The burden of thinking, and let me go drinking
   The careless pleasures of youth's bright hours?
If silver threads from my tresses vanish,
   If a glow once more in my pale cheek gleams,
Wilt thou slay duty and give back the beauty
   Of days untroubled by aught but dreams?

When the soft, fair arms of the siren Summer
   Encircle the earth in their languorous fold.
Will vast, deep oceans of sweet emotions
   Surge through my veins as they surged of old?
Canst thou bring back from a day long vanished
   The leaping pulse and the boundless aim?
I will pay thee double for all thy trouble,
   If thou wilt restore all these, good dame.

CONFESSION

I

How shall a maid make answer to a man
Who summons her, by love's supreme decree,
To open her whole heart, that he may see
The intricate strange ways that love began.
So many streams from that great fountain ran
To feed the river that now rushes free,
So deep the heart, so full of mystery;
How shall a maid make answer to a man?

If I turn back each leaflet of my heart,
And let your eyes scan all the records there,
Of dreams of love that came before I knew,
Though in those dreams you had no place or part,
Yet, know that each emotion was a stair
Which led my ripening womanhood to you.

II

Nay, I was not insensate till you came;
I know man likes to think a woman clay,
Devoid of feeling till the warming ray
Sent from his heart lights her with sudden flame.
You asked for truth; I answer without shame;
My human heart pulsed blood by night and day,
And I believed that Love had come my way
Before he conquered with your face and name.

I do not know when first I felt this fire
That lends such lustre to my hopes and fears,
And burns a pathway to you with each thought.
I think in that great hour when God's desire
For worlds to love flung forth a million spheres,
This miracle of love in me was wrought.

An open door, a moonlit sky,
A child-like maid with musing eye,
A manly footstep passing by.

Light as a dewdrop falls from space
Upon a rosebud's folded grace,
A kiss fell on her girlish face.

"Good-night, good-bye," and he was gone.
And so was childhood; it was dawn
In that young heart the moon shone on.

His name? his face? dim memories;
I only know in that first kiss
Was prophesied this later bliss.

The dreams within my bosom grew;
Nay, grieve not that my tale is true,
Since all those dreams led straight to you.

One time when Autumn donned her robes of splendour
And rustled down the year's receding track,
As I passed dreaming by, a voice all tender
Haled me with youth's soft call to linger back.
I turned and listened to a golden story!
A wondrous tale, half human, half divine—
A page from bright September's book of glory,
To memorise and make forever mine.

Strange argosies from passion's unknown oceans
Cruised down my veins, a vague elusive fleet,
With foreign cargoes of unnamed emotions,
While wafts of song blew shoreward, dim and sweet,
And sleeping still (because unwaked by you)
I dreamed and dreamed, and thought my visions true.
I woke when all the crimson colour faded
And wanton Autumn's lips and cheeks were pale;
And when the sorrowing year had slowly waded,
With failing footsteps, through the snow-filled vale.
I woke and knew the glamour of a season
Had lent illusive lustre to a dream,
And looking in the clear calm eyes of Reason,
I smiled and said, "Farewell to things that seem."
'Twas but a red leaf from a lush September
The wind of dreams across my pathway blew,
But oh! my love! the whole round year remember,
With all its seasons I bestow on you.
The red leaf perished in the first cold blast
The full year's harvests at your feet I cast.

L'ENVOI

Absolve me, prince; confession is all over.
But listen and take warning, oh! my lover.
You put to rout all dreams that may have been;
You won the day, but 'tis not all to win;
Guard well the fort, lest new dreams enter in.

A MARRIED COQUETTE

Sit still, I say, and dispense with heroics!
  I hurt your wrists? Well, you have hurt me.
It is time you found out that all men are not stoics,
  Nor toys to be used as your mood may be.
I will not let go of your hands, nor leave you
  Until I have spoken. No man, you say,
Dared ever so treat you before? I believe you,
  For you have dealt only with boys till to-day.

You women lay stress on your fine perception,
  Your intuitions are prated about;
You claim an occult sort of conception
  Of matters which men must reason out.
So then, of course, when you ask me kindly
  "To call again soon," you read my heart.
I cannot believe you were acting blindly;
  You saw my passion for you from the start.

You are one of those women who charm without trying;
  The clay you are made of is magnet ore,
And I am the steel; yet, there's no denying
  You led me to loving you more and more.
You are fanning a flame that may burn too brightly,
  Oft easily kindled, but hard to put out;
I am not a man to be played with lightly,
  To come at a gesture and go at a pout.

A brute you call me, a creature inhuman;
  You say I insult you, and bid me go.

And you? Oh, you are a saintly woman,
　　With thoughts as pure as the drifted snow.
Pah! you are but one of a thousand beauties
　　Who think they are living exemplary lives:
They break no commandments, and do all their duties
　　As Christian women and spotless wives.

But with drooping of lids, and lifting of faces,
　　And baring of shoulders, and well-timed sighs,
And the devil knows what other subtle graces,
　　You are mental wantons, who sin with the eyes.
You lure love to wake, yet bid it keep under,
　　You tempt us to fall, but bid reason control;
And then you are full of an outraged wonder
　　When we get to wanting you, body and soul.

Why, look at yourself! You were no stranger
　　To the fact that my heart was already on fire.
When you asked me to call you knew my danger,
　　Yet here you are, dressed in the gown I admire;
For half of the evil on earth is invented
　　By vain, pretty women with nothing to do
But to keep themselves manicured, powdered, and scented,
　　And seek for sensations amusing and new.

But when I play at love at a lady's commanding,
　　I always am certain to win one game;
So there—there—there! I will leave my branding
　　On the lips that are free now to cry "Shame, shame!"
You hate me? Quite likely! It does not surprise me,
　　Brute force? I confess it; but still you were kissed;
And one thing is certain—you cannot despise me
　　For having been played with, controlled, and dismissed.

And the next time you see that a man is attracted
　　By the beauty and graces that are not for him,

Don't lead him on to be half distracted;
  Keep out of deep waters although you can swim.
For when he is caught in the whirlpool of passion,
  Where many bold swimmers are seen to drown,
A man will reach out and, in desperate fashion,
  Will drag whoever is nearest him down.

Though the strings of his heart may be wrenched and riven
  By a maiden coquette who has led him along,
She can be pardoned, excused, and forgiven,
  For innocence blindfolded walks into wrong.
But she who has willingly taken the fetter
  That Cupid forges at Hymen's command—
Well, she is the woman who ought to know better;
  She needs no mercy at any man's hand.

In the game of hearts, though a woman be winner,
  The odds are ever against her, you know;
The world is ready to call her a sinner,
  And man is ready to make her so.
Shame is likely, and sorrow is certain,
  And the man has the best of it, end as it may.
So now, my lady, we'll drop the curtain,
  And put out the lights. We are through with our play.

FORBIDDEN SPEECH

The passion you forbade my lips to utter
   Will not be silenced. You must hear it in
The sullen thunders when they roll and mutter:
   And when the tempest nears, with wail and din,
I know your calm forgetfulness is broken,
And to your heart you whisper, "He has spoken."

All nature understands and sympathises
   With human passion. When the restless sea
Turns in its futile search for peace, and rises
   To plead and to pursue, it pleads for me.
And with each desperate billow's anguished fretting.
Your heart must tell you, "He is not forgetting."

When unseen hands in lightning strokes are writing
   Mysterious words upon a cloudy scroll,
Know that my pent-up passion is inditing
   A cypher message for your woman's soul;
And when the lawless winds rush by you shrieking,
Let your heart say, "Now his despair is speaking."

Love comes, nor goes, at beck or call of reason,
   Nor is love silent—though it says no word;
By day or night, in any clime or season,
   A dominating passion must be heard.
So shall you hear, through Junes and through Decembers,
The voice of Nature saying, "He remembers."

THE SUMMER GIRL

She's the jauntiest of creatures, she's the daintiest of misses,
With her pretty patent leathers or her alligator ties,
With her eyes inviting glances and her lips inviting kisses,
As she wanders by the ocean or strolls under country skies.

She's a captivating dresser, and her parasols are stunning;
Her fads will take your breath away, her hats are dreams of style;
She is not so very bookish, but with repartee and punning
She can set the savants laughing and make even dudelets smile.

She has no attacks of talent, she is not a stage-struck maiden;
She is wholly free from hobbies, and she dreams of no "career";
She is mostly gay and happy, never sad or care-beladen,
Though she sometimes sighs a little if a gentleman is near.

She's a sturdy little walker and she braves all kinds of weather,
And when the rain or fog or mist drive rival crimps a-wreck,
Her fluffy hair goes curling like a kinked-up ostrich feather
Around her ears and forehead and the white nape of her neck.

She is like a fish in water; she can handle reins and racket;
From head to toe and finger-tips she's thoroughly alive;
When she goes promenading in a most distracting jacket,
The rustle round her feet suggests how laundresses may thrive.

She can dare the wind and sunshine in the most bravado manner,
And after hours of sailing she has merely cheeks of rose;

Old Sol himself seems smitten, and at most will only tan her,
Though to everybody else he gives a danger-signal nose.

She's a trifle sentimental, and she's fond of admiration,
And she sometimes flirts a little in the season's giddy whirl;
But win her if you can, sir, she may prove your life's salvation,
For an angel masquerading oft is she, the Summer Girl.

THE GHOST

Through the open door of dreamland
Came a ghost of long ago, long ago.
When I wakened, all unheeding
Was the phantom to my pleading;
For he would not turn and go,
But beside me all the day,
In my work and in my play,
Trod this ghost of long ago, long ago.

Not a vague and pallid phantom
Was this ghost that came to me, followed me:
Though he rose from regions haunted,
Though he came unbid, unwanted,
He was very fair to see.
Like the radiant sun in space
Was the halo round the face
Of that ghost that came to me, followed me.

And he wore no shroud or cere-cloth
As he wandered at my side, close beside:
He was clothed in royal splendour
And his eyes were deep and tender,
While he walked in stately pride;
And he seemed like some great king,
Not afraid of anything,
As he wandered at my side, close beside.

Then I turned to him commanding
That he go the way he came, whence he came.

93

But he answered me in sorrow,
"May the Past not seek to borrow
From the Present without blame—
Just one memory from its store,
Ere it goes to come no more,
Back the pathway that it came, whence it came?"

Then ashamed of my full coffers,
I gave forth from Memory's hold (wondrous hold!)
All I owed of tax and duty
For remembered hours of beauty,
Which I paid in thoughts of gold;
Yet my present seemed to be
Richer still for all the fee
I gave forth from Memory's hold (wondrous hold!).

THE SIGNBOARD

I will paint you a sign, rumseller,
    And hang it above your door;
A truer and better signboard
    Than ever you had before.
I will paint with the skill of a master,
    And many shall pause to see
This wonderful piece of painting,
    So like the reality.

I will paint yourself, rumseller,
    As you wait for that fair young boy,
Just in the morning of manhood,
    A mother's pride and joy.
He has no thought of stopping,
    But you greet him with a smile,
And you seem so blithe and friendly,
    That he pauses to chat awhile.

I will paint you again, rumseller,
    I will paint you as you stand,
With a foaming glass of liquor
    Extended in your hand.
He wavers, but you urge him—
    Drink, pledge me just this one!
And he takes the glass and drains it,
    And the hellish work is done.

And next I will paint a drunkard—
    Only a year has flown,

But into that loathsome creature
　　The fair young boy has grown.
The work was sure and rapid.
　　I will paint him as he lies
In a torpid, drunken slumber,
　　Under the wintry skies.

I will paint the form of the mother
　　As she kneels at her darling's side,
Her beautiful boy that was dearer
　　Than all the world beside.
I will paint the shape of a coffin,
　　Labelled with one word—"Lost"
I will paint all this, rumseller,
　　And will paint it free of cost.

The sin and the shame and the sorrow,
　　The crime and the want and the woe
That are born there in your workshop,
　　No hand can paint, you know.
But I'll paint you a sign, rumseller,
　　And many shall pause to view
This wonderful swinging signboard,
　　So terribly, fearfully true.

A MAN'S REPENTANCE

(Intended for recitation at club dinners)

To-night when I came from the club at eleven,
  Under the gaslight I saw a face—
A woman's face! and I swear to heaven
  It looked like the ghastly ghost of—Grace!

And Grace? why, Grace was fair; and I tarried,
  And loved her a season as we men do.
And then—but pshaw! why, of course, she is married,
  Has a husband, and doubtless a babe or two.

She was perfectly calm on the day we parted;
  She spared me a scene, to my great surprise.
"She wasn't the kind to be broken-hearted,"
  I remember she said, with a spark in her eyes.

I was tempted, I know, by her proud defiance,
  To make good my promise there and then.
But the world would have called it a mésalliance!
  I dreaded the comments and sneers of men.

So I left her to grieve for a faithless lover,
  And to hide her heart from the cold world's sight
As women do hide them, the wide earth over;
  My God! was it Grace that I saw to-night?

I thought of her married, and often with pity,
  A poor man's wife in some dull place.

And now to know she is here in the city,
  Under the gaslight, and with that face!

Yet I knew it at once, in spite of the daubing
  Of paint and powder, and she knew me;
She drew a quick breath that was almost sobbing
  And shrank in the shade so I should not see.

There was hell in her eyes! She was worn and jaded
  Her soul is at war with the life she has led.
As I looked on that face so strangely faded
  I wonder God did not strike me dead.

While I have been happy and gay and jolly,
  Received by the very best people in town,
That girl whom I led in the way to folly,
  Has gone on recklessly down and down.

                    * * *

Two o'clock, and no sleep has found me;
  That face I saw in the street-lamp's light
Peers everywhere out from the shadows around me—
  I know how a murderer feels to-night.

ARISTARCHUS

(THE NAME OF THE MOUNTAIN IN THE MOON)

It was long and long ago our love began;
  It is something all unmeasured by time's span:
In an era and a spot, by the Modern World forgot,
  We were lovers, ere God named us, Maid and Man.

Like the memory of music made by streams,
  All the beauty of that other love life seems;
But I always thought it so, and at last I know, I know,
  We were lovers in the Land of Silver Dreams.

When the moon was at the full, I found the place;
  Out and out, across the seas of shining space,
On a quest that could not fail, I unfurled my memory's sail
  And cast anchor in the Bay of Love's First Grace.

At the foot of Aristarchus lies this bay,
  (Oh! the wonder of that mountain far away!)
And the Land of Silver Dreams all about it shines and gleams,
  Where we loved before God fashioned night or day.

We were souls, in eerie bodies made of light;
  We were winged, and we could speed from height to height;
And we built a nest called Hope, on the sheer Moon Mountain
Slope,
  Where we sat, and watched new worlds wheel into sight.

And we saw this little planet known as Earth,
    When the mighty Mother Chaos gave it birth;
But in love's conceit we thought all those worlds from space were
brought,
    For no greater aim or purpose than our mirth.

    And we laughed in love's abandon, and we sang,
    Till the echoing peals of Aristarchus rang,
As hot hissing comets came, and white suns burst into flame,
    And a myriad worlds from out the darkness sprang.

    I can show you, when the Moon is at its best,
    Aristarchus, and the spot we made our nest,
Oh! I always wondered why, when the Moon was in the sky,
    I was stirred with such strange longing, and unrest.

    And I knew the subtle beauty and the force
    Of our love was never bounded by Earth's course.
So with Memory's sail unfurled, I went cruising past this world,
    And I followed till I traced it to its source.

DELL AND I

In a mansion grand, just over the way
   Lives bonny, beautiful Dell;
You may have heard of this lady gay,
   For she is a famous belle.
I live in a low cot opposite—
   You never have heard of me;
For when the lady moon shines bright,
   Who would a pale star see?
But ah, well! ah, well! I am happier far than Dell,
   As strange as that may be.

Dell has robes of the richest kind—
   Pinks and purples and blues;
And she worries her maid and frets her mind
   To know which one to choose.
Which shall it be now, silk or lace?
   In which will I be most fair?
She stands by the mirror with anxious face,
   And her maid looks on in despair.
Ah, well! ah, well! I am not worried, you see, like Dell,
   For I have but one to wear.

Dell has lovers of every grade,
   Of every age and style;
Suitors flutter about the maid,
   And bask in her word and smile.
She keeps them all, with a coquette's art,
   As suits her mood or mirth,

And vainly wonders if in one heart
   Of all true love has birth.
Ah, well! ah, well! I never question myself like Dell,
   For I know a true heart's worth.

Pleasure to Dell seems stale and old,
   Often she sits and sighs;
Life to me is a tale untold,
   Each day is a glad surprise.
Dell will marry, of course, some day,
   After her belleship is run;
She will cavil the matter in worldly way
   And wed Dame Fortune's son
But, ah, well! sweet to tell, I shall not dally and choose like
Dell,
   For I love and am loved by—one.

ABOUT MAY

One night Nurse Sleep held out her hand
  To tired little May.
"Come, go with me to Wonderland,"
  She said, "I know the way.
Just rock-a-by—hum-m-m,
  And lo! we come
To the place where the dream-girls play."

But naughty May, she wriggled away
  From Sleep's soft arms, and said:
"I must stay awake till I eat my cake,
  And then I will go to bed;
With a by-lo, away I will go."
  But the good nurse shook her head.

She shook her head and away she sped,
  While May sat munching her crumb.
But after the cake there came an ache,
  Though May cried: "Come, Sleep, come,
And it's oh! my! let us by-lo-by"—
  All save the echoes were dumb.

She ran after Sleep toward Wonderland,
  Ran till the morning light;
And just as she caught her and grasped her hand,
  A nightmare gave her a fright.
And it's by-lo, I hope she'll know
  Better another night.

VANITY FAIR

In Vanity Fair, as we bow and smile,
  As we talk of the opera after the weather,
As we chat of fashion and fad and style,
  We know we are playing a part together.
You know that the mirth she wears, she borrows;
She knows you laugh but to hide your sorrows;
We know that under the silks and laces,
And back of beautiful, beaming faces,
Lie secret trouble and grim despair,
      In Vanity Fair.

In Vanity Fair, on dress parade,
  Our colours look bright and our swords are gleaming;
But many a uniform's worn and frayed,
  And most of the weapons, despite their seeming,
Are dull and blunted and badly battered,
And close inspection will show how tattered
And stained are the banners that float above us.
Our comrades hate, while they swear to love us;
And robed like Pleasure walks gaunt-eyed Care,
      In Vanity Fair.

In Vanity Fair, as we strive for place,
  As we rush and jostle and crowd and hurry,
We know the goal is not worth the race—
  We know the prize is not worth the worry;
That all our gain means loss for another;
That in fighting for self we wound each other;
That the crown of success weighs hard and presses

The brow of the victor with thorns—not caresses;
That honours are empty and worthless to wear,
    In Vanity Fair.

But in Vanity Fair, as we pass along,
  We meet strong hearts that are worth the knowing
'Mong poor paste jewels that deck the throng,
  We see a solitaire sometimes glowing.
We find grand souls under robes of fashion,
'Neath light demeanours hide strength and passion;
And fair fine honour and godlike resistance
In halls of pleasure may have existence;
And we find pure altars and shrines of prayer
    In Vanity Fair.

THE GIDDY GIRL

[This recitation is intended to be given with an accompaniment of waltz music, introducing dance-steps at the refrain "With one, two, three," etc.]

A giddy young maiden with nimble feet,
Heigh-ho! alack and alas!
Declared she would far rather dance than eat,
And the truth of it came to pass.
For she danced all day and she danced all night;
She danced till the green earth faded white;
She danced ten partners out of breath;
She danced the eleventh one quite to death;
And still she redowaed up and down—
The giddiest girl in town.
With one, two, three; one, two, three; one, two, three—kick;
Chassée back, chassée back, whirl around quick.
The name of this damsel ended with E—
  Heigh-ho; alack and a-day!
And she was as fair as a maiden need be,
  Till she danced her beauty away.
She danced her big toes out of joint;
She danced her other toes all to a point;
She danced out slipper and boot and shoe;
She danced till the bones of her feet came through.
And still she redowaed, waltzed, and whirled—
The giddiest girl in the world.
With one, two, three; one, two, three; one, two, three—kick;
Chassée back, chassée back, whirl around quick.

106

Now the end of my story is sad to relate—
   Heigh-ho! and away we go!
For this beautiful maiden's final fate
   Is shrouded in gloom and woe.
She danced herself into a patent top;
She whirled and whirled till she could not stop;
She danced and bounded and sprang so far,
That she stuck at last on a pointed star;
And there she must dance till the Judgment Day,
And after it, too, for she danced away

Her soul, you see, so she has no place anywhere out of space,

With her one, two, three; one, two, three; one, two, three—kick;

Chassée back, chassée back, whirl about quick.

A GIRL'S AUTUMN REVERIE

We plucked a red rose, you and I,
  All in the summer weather;
Sweet its perfume and rare its bloom,
  Enjoyed by us together.
The rose is dead, the summer fled,
  And bleak winds are complaining;
We dwell apart, but in each heart
  We find the thorn remaining.

We sipped a sweet wine, you and I,
  All in the summer weather.
The beaded draught we lightly quaffed,
  And filled the glass together.
Together we watched its rosy glow,
  And saw its bubbles glitter;
Apart, alone we only know
  The lees are very bitter.

We walked in sunshine, you and I,
  All in the summer weather:
The very night seemed noonday bright,
  When we two were together.
I wonder why with our good-bye
  O'er hill and vale and meadow
There fell such shade, our paths seemed laid
  For evermore in shadow.

We dreamed a sweet dream, you and I,
  All in the summer weather,
Where rose and wine and warm sunshine

Were mingled in together.
We dreamed that June was with us yet,
  We woke to find December.
We dreamed that we two could forget,
  We woke but to remember.

HIS YOUTH

"Dying? I am not dying? Are you mad?
   You think I need to ask for heavenly grace?
I think you are a fiend, who would be glad
   To see me struggle in death's cold embrace.

"But, man, you lie! for I am strong—in truth
   Stronger than I have been in years; and soon
I shall feel young again as in my youth,
   My glorious youth—life's one great priceless boon.

"O youth, youth, youth! O God! that golden time,
   When proud and glad I laughed the hours away.
Why, there's no sacrifice (perhaps no crime)
   I'd pause at, could it make me young to-day.

"But I'm not old! I grew—just ill, somehow;
   Grew stiff of limb, and weak, and dim of sight.
It was but sickness. I am better now,
   Oh, vastly better, ever since last night.

"And I could weep warm floods of happy tears
   To think my strength is coming back at last,
For I have dreamed of such an hour for years,
   As I lay thinking of my glorious past.

"You shake your head? Why, man, if you were sane
   I'd strike you to my feet, I would, in truth.
How dare you tell me that my hopes are vain?

How dare you say I have outlived my youth?

"'In heaven I may regain it'? Oh, be still!
  I want no heaven but what my glad youth gave.
Its long, bright hours, its rapture and its thrill—
  O youth, youth, youth! it is my youth I crave.

"There is no heaven! There's nothing but a deep
  And yawning grave from which I shrink in fear.
I am not sure of even rest or sleep;
  Perhaps we lie and think as I have here.

"Think, think, think, think, as we lie there and rot,
  And hear the young above us laugh in glee.
How dare you say I'm dying! I am not.
  I would curse God if such a thing could be.

"Why, see me stand! why, hear this strong, full breath—
  Dare you repeat that silly, base untruth?"
A cry—a fall—the silence known as death
  Hushed his wild words. Well, has he found his youth?

UNDER THE SHEET

What a terrible night! Does the Night, I wonder—
  The Night, with her black veil down to her feet
Like an ordained nun, know what lies under
  That awful, motionless, snow-white sheet?
The winds seem crazed, and, wildly howling,
  Over the sad earth blindly go.
Do they and the dark clouds over them scowling,
  Do they dream or know?

Why, here in the room, not a week or over—
  Tho' it must be a week, not more than one—
(I cannot recken of late or discover
  When one day is ended or one begun),
But here in this room we were laughing lightly,
  And glad was the measure our two hearts beat;
And the royal face that was smiling so brightly
  Lies under that sheet.

I know not why—it is strange and fearful,
  But I am afraid of her, lying there;
She who was always so gay and cheerful,
  Lying so still with that stony stare:
She who was so like some grand sultana,
  Fond of colour and glow and heat,
To lie there clothed in that awful manner
  In a stark white sheet.

She who was made out of summer blisses,
  Tropical, beautiful, gracious, fair,
To lie and stare at my fondest kisses—

God! no wonder it whitens my hair
Shriek, O wind! for the world is lonely;
   Trail cloud-veil to the nun Night's feet!
For all that I prize in life is only
   A shape and a sheet.

A PIN

Oh! I know a certain woman who is reckoned with the good,
But she fills me with more terror than a raging lion could.
The little chills run up and down my spine whene'er we meet,
Though she seems a gentle creature and she's very trim and neat.

And she has a thousand virtues and not one acknowledged sin,
But she is the sort of person you could liken to a pin.
And she pricks you, and she sticks you, in a way that can't be
said—
When you seek for what has hurt you, why, you cannot find the
head.

But she fills you with discomfort and exasperating pain—
If anybody asks you why, you really can't explain.
A pin is such a tiny thing—of that there is no doubt—
Yet when it's sticking in your flesh, you're wretched till it's out!

She is wonderfully observing. When she meets a pretty girl
She is always sure to tell her if her "bang" is out of curl.
And she is so sympathetic; to her friend who's much admired,
She is often heard remarking: "Dear, you look so worn and tired!"

And she is a careful critic; for on yesterday she eyed
The new dress I was airing with a woman's natural pride,
And she said: "Oh, how becoming!" and then softly added, "It
Is really a misfortune that the basque is such a fit."

Then she said: "If you had heard me yestereve, I'm sure, my friend,
You would say I am a champion who knows how to defend."

And she left me with a feeling—most unpleasant, I aver—
That the whole world would despise me if it hadn't been for her.

Whenever I encounter her, in such a nameless way
She gives me the impression I am at my worst that day;
And the hat that was imported (and that cost me half a sonnet)
With just one glance from her round eyes becomes a Bowery
bonnet.

She is always bright and smiling, sharp and shining for a thrust;
Use does not seem to blunt her point, nor does she gather rust.
Oh! I wish some hapless specimen of mankind would begin
To tidy up the world for me, by picking up this pin.

THE COMING MAN

Oh! not for the great departed,
  Who formed our country's laws,
And not for the bravest-hearted,
  Who died in freedom's cause,
And not for some living hero
  To whom all bend the knee,
My muse would raise her song of praise—
  But for the man to be.

For out of the strife which woman
  Is passing through to-day,
A man that is more than human
  Shall yet be born, I say.
A man in whose pure spirit
  No dross of self will lurk;
A man who is strong to cope with wrong,
  A man who is proud to work.

A man with hope undaunted,
  A man with godlike power,
Shall come when he most is wanted,
  Shall come at the needed hour.
He shall silence the din and clamour
  Of clan disputing with clan,
And toil's long fight with purse-proud might
  Shall triumph through this man.

I know he is coming, coming,
  To help, to guide, to save.

Though I hear no martial drumming,
   And see no flags that wave.
But the great soul travail of woman,
   And the bold free thought unfurled,
Are heralds that say he is on the way—
   The coming man of the world.

Mourn not for vanished ages,
   With their great heroic men,
Who dwell in history's pages
   And live in the poet's pen.
For the grandest times are before us,
   And the world is yet to see
The noblest worth of this old earth
   In the men that are to be.

www.ingramcontent.com/pod-product-compliance
Lightning Source LLC
Chambersburg PA
CBHW031948070426
42453CB00007BA/513